What Next

Eileen DiStasio-Clark

With Great Love and Appreciation to those who Have and Do Bless My Life

My Family:

Joseph DeStasio Sr. & Miriam Lucille Baragone DeStasio, My Late Parents.

Andrea Jean DeStasio McIntosh, My Older Sister and their Family.

Joseph DeStasio Jr., My Younger and Only Brother and their Family.

Donna Marie DeStasio Wagner, My Younger Sister and their Family.

My Children:

Eileen, Rebekah, Rachel, S. Michael, Jennifer, Sharon, Tara, Stephanie, Apryll, Mikaelah, & M. Trevor and THEIR Families!!

ACKNOWLEDGEMENTS

First and foremost, I express, deeply, my sincere gratitude to our Heavenly Father for blessing me with the gift and talent of writing! I know I could not do what I do without His assistance.

I also want to acknowledge and express gratitude to the members of my birth family—Joseph Sr., Miriam, Andrea, Joseph Junior, and Donna. All the experiences of my childhood years, experiences that taught me so very much and enabled me to reveal my true self to myself, came about through my experiences and relationships with them.

And, of course, it goes without saying, but I will say it anyway: I also want to acknowledge and note my gratitude to my children, Eileen, Rebekah, Rachel, S. Michael, Jennifer, Sharon, Tara, Stephanie, Apryll, Mikaelah, and M. Trevor, and their families! Through multiple things they said to me, over multiple years, I finally came to the realization that Heavenly Father gave me the gift of writing and opened the doors to these experiences because He knew that by sharing them with others, others could feel His love too.

And He definitely wants us all to know that He, Heavenly Father, Heavenly Mother, and Jehovah truly do loves us!!!

INTRODUCTION

There are sixteen books in this series, which I refer to as *"The Ellie Series."* All of the characters in these stories portray real people from my life. The main characters depict the members of my family: Daddy is my daddy; Mommy is my mommy; Jeannie is my older sister; Junior is my brother; Maria is my younger sister; and Ellie is me. Now, those are not our actual first names, but they do reference us.

The first story in the series presents our Heavenly Father's Plan of Salvation and takes place in the Pre-Earth World. Now, of course, because we all—when we were born—received what is known as The Veil of Forgetfulness, I do not actually remember everything from or about the Pre-Earth World, but I do know about and understand it from much study and worship as a member of The Church of Jesus Christ of Latter-Day Saints, and memories restored to me through the Holy Spirit. So, from this story there is much truth to be learned.

The last story in the series is set in the Post-Mortal World, and presents a depiction of what happens to us after this life. Again, because I have not gone there yet, I cannot say I 'remember' this. But, I have also learned about the Post-Mortal World from much study and worship as a member of The Church of Jesus Christ of Latter-Day Saints.

All of the other stories are based on true events from my life; events that actually occurred when and how they are depicted in these stories. I chose these events because they are among the many occurrences in my life that presented, or revealed that which I already knew without having to be taught, Principles of Eternal Truths.

Also, I chose these events as the settings for my stories because they depict wonderful learning moments from my childhood and adolescent years, lessons that have blessed and benefited me throughout the whole of my life and will forever continue to do so. Also, through these great truths and their consequences in my life, I have been able to share them with many others, whose lives have also been blessed by them.

So, please read and enjoy, then care and share the messages and stories with others!!

Now, there are also a couple of things you can look for:

In each story, the title of the previous story is presented in *italicized* form, the title of the next story is presented in *Capitalized Italicized* form, and the title of the story being read is presented in **emboldened** form.

Also, every story has at least one word that is uncommon or 'created.'

So, as you read, search, find, and have fun!

WHAT NEXT

It must have been a longer time than it felt like it had been. It must have been far more full of activities and adventures than just what was popping up in Ellie's mind. Afterall, it had been thirteen years, and now it was over.

'What was over?' you may be wondering. I will tell you what was over; school was over.

It was Wednesday, June 9, 1971. Ellie had graduated from high school the day before, on June 8, and now she was sitting in their Catalpa tree, wondering what she would do next.

She thought about all of the things she had gotten herself involved in during her high school years: sports—Field Hockey and Basketball, music—Junior Chorus, McDowell Chorus, County Chorus, a bunch of different clubs—Future Homemakers of America, Future Teachers of America, Future Nurses of America, Model UN, Y-Teens, International Student Committee, the Dramatic Club, Theater, the Library Club, the Health Careers Club, the Chess Club, the... well, I am sure you get the idea. She did a lot of different things, not just learn everything she could learn. Why, she was even a Public Address Announcer! Yes, she most definitely had gotten herself involved in everything that she could, and as she thought about them, she considered, with a heap of gratitude, all the gifts, talents, and knowledge they had provided for her. But she was still rather confused about where to go and what to do next.

She pondered over all of the things she had told herself she wanted to pursue and why she changed her mind about them. For one thing, Ellie had thought she wanted to go into acting. She had very much enjoyed being in all the plays and skits that she had taken part in. But, after learning more about what goes on in that world, she quickly learned that it was not a world for her! She had also thought she wanted to be a professional singer. But again, she came to realize that that world was no different from the acting world. So, of course, that could not happen either.

She thought about horsemanship and, of course, that surprised no one. After all, Ellie not only loved to ride, train, and take care of horses, but she still believed, or maybe just wondered if God really did put the horses in this world because she wanted them here. Now, of course, Ellie did not see how that could be possible, either. After all, she did not even have a horse of her own. You see, while the Stations lived sufficiently, they had never had enough extra money for Ellie to get a horse and board it at a stable. So she did not see that as something she could do, and besides, she most definitely did not want to do something that would take her away from her family! Nope!!! No way!!!! Family was just far too important to her for her to do that.

Of course, she also considered teaching, which she knew she would very much enjoy, but... well... she was not really sure what she felt about that one. You see, even though schools were still pretty good then, she could see some changes occurring that she did not support and would not promote!

She thought she had made the right choice when she chose to become a nun, even though she knew that she did not really want to do that because Ellie really did not want to be separated from her family, and she definitely wanted a family of her own! Nonetheless, because she thought that was what God would want her to do at least that is what her Catechism teachers had said. She had decided to do that. But, because that choice had made, not only her, but her daddy sad, and because he had asked her to wait until she was eighteen to make that decision, she was not really sure it would ever happen.

Uh, **Side Note:** Because Ellie was seventeen when she graduated that 'wait' would be three months, so she decided to study the Bible, the whole Bible, which she had never really done before, and the history of the Catholic Church as a way to prepare herself to enter the convent when she was eighteen. However, the more she read, the more confused she became. It was becoming rather clear to her that much of what she had been taught in Catechism was not what was being taught in the Bible, and she was not comfortable with that. Now, back to the other side.

Of course, she did know that what she really preferred was to get married and have her own children! That is most definitely what she would give up everything else for, as long as God said that was what was right for her. And that was what she needed to know, what He said was right for her! So, that was why she was sitting in their Catalpa tree, talking to the angels.

She told them how much she had enjoyed all the service projects she had helped with through the Y-Teens organization. From that experience, she knew she wanted to spend her life serving, but how and to whom?

She explained to them that she had really loved working in the high school and elementary school libraries. In fact, she had loved that so much that she did it all four years that she was in high school. Well, wait a minute! She actually only worked in the elementary school library when she was in ninth and tenth grades because after that, when her school, West Reading High, merged with the neighboring school, Wyomissing High, they were too far away from the nearest elementary school for the Library Club kids to work there. Anyway, whether they were in the high school or the elementary school, she loved the libraries. But as a career; she did not think that would be a good match for her.

From her involvement in the Future Homemakers, Future Teachers, and Future Nurses' clubs, she learned again what she already knew, and that was that what she most wanted to be was a mother—of 200 kids—well at least a mother of twelve boys and three girls. But she could not do that until she got married and could have children. So what she would do until then, was the question that was perplexing her mind.

From all her other experiences in school, Public Address, Chess Club, the school newspaper staff... well, just everything, one thing she did know was that she really wanted to go to college. In fact, she had applied to fifteen different colleges in the United States and Europe, and she had been accepted to all of them. But she had chosen to go to none of them.

"Why?!" you are probably asking with surprise. Well, I will tell you why.

Ellie might tell you that she really did not know if she knew why she did not select one to attend. But I am pretty sure it was because the ones that most intrigued her, were either too expensive or too far away. Being a want-to-be-close-to-home kind of kid, distance mattered to her, and while her family lived well, they were not rich, so cost mattered too. The colleges that were closer to home or were less costly did not really appeal to Ellie. She could not tell herself why but she knew that they did not. So, she had not chosen any college to go to.

And, of course, as I already explained, the one thing that Ellie most wanted to do, and would do, was whatever it was that God told her to do. Now, because she could not tell herself that she actually knew what that was. Ellie was sitting in their Catalpa tree, on the biggest branch in the middle of the tree, leaning against Catalpa's big twisty trunk, and thinking, thinking, thin... well, you know what she was doing.

In fact, she was not just thinking; she was also asking the angels, "**What next?**"

After a bit of time had passed, Ellie heard Mommy call her name. "Ellie," Mommy called from the kitchen window, "dinner is ready. Come down out of Catalpa and go get your brother. He is at Mik's house. Make it quick; the rest of us are already ready to sit down at the table."

"Okay," Ellie replied as she began to climb down out of Catalpa. Once on the ground, she ran through the yard, out the back gate, and across the alley, which was really Grape Street, to Mik's house. She knocked on the door with a rhythm that would make anyone think she was playing the drums, and called, in a tone that sounded like she was singing, "Junior, it is time to come home; dinner is ready."

As soon as Junior came through the door and said, "I will beat you this time," they both began running. It was what they always did—raced each other—but just for fun. It never mattered to either of them who got to... wherever they were going... first. They both cheered as if they both had won.

But that was something to be expected from them. You see, ever since Junior was born, when Ellie was three years old, well actually, he was born two months and one week before she turned three, but that was close enough to say she was three, anyway, ever since then, they were best friends. In fact, Ellie always told everyone that they were not just best friends here, on earth, but they had become best friends even before they were born.

Okay, so now, when everyone was in their seats at the table, Daddy offered the blessing on the food and Mommy filled their plates. She put shepherd's pie, kernels of corn, and a bit of salad on their main course plate, filled their glasses with water, and placed a few pizzelles on each dessert plate. As they always did during dinner, and as they ate their dinner, they shared with one another the tales of their day.

Jeannie went first. "Well," Jeannie began, "I did not have the best of days. I mean, nothing really went wrong, I just do not enjoy fixing people's hair as much as I used to think I would. In fact, I do not think I like it at all!"

Side Note:** Clora, a cousin to the Stations' kids, was a beautician. She had her salon in the living room of Nonna Rabgaeno's house. Anytime the Stations went to Nonna's, when Clora was working, they would watch everything she did and then, when they went home, they would try to do what they had seen her do. From that, Jeannie had thought that she would like to be a beautician too. So, about a year or maybe a half, after she graduated from high school, she started beauty school, but that was what she was not enjoying. Now, back to the other side.

"I do not know if I really want to continue," Jeannie added, "but I will if I have to."

"Why do you think you would not want to continue?" Ellie asked with a tiny bit of surprise. "That is what you always said you wanted to do."

"I know," Jeannie replied, "but it is not quite what I thought it would be. I really do not think I would enjoy it. Most of the women whose hair I have fixed at school were just so grumpy. And no matter how much I tried to please them, they just kept complaining about this, that, and everything else I did. Besides, I get bored doing the same things over and over. I really do not like washing other people's hair. And wrapping it around the curlers is a pain, especially when their hair is rather short. In fact, I do not think I can think of anything that I actually like about being a beautician."

After a small moment of silence, Mommy said, "Jeannie, you do not have to continue beauty school if you do not like fixing hair. There is no point in putting all that time and money into something you will probably not end up doing."

"Oh," Jeannie replied, with a little bit of surprise, "I thought you would tell me I should just stick with it. If you are really okay with me giving it up, I will!!"

Side Note Number Two: Jeannie did end up getting out of the program a few months later. Then she got a job at a utility company, working in the office. Now, back to the other side again.

Ellie was next to share her daily report. But she really did not have too much to say because she had not done too much that day. After all, she spent most of it trying to figure out what she wanted to do now that she had graduated from high school. After she explained that to her family, she said, "But I did make one decision; I am going to get a job. I think I want to apply for a job at John Wannamaker's Department Store. I like that store." Then directing her question to Daddy, she asked, "Do you think that would be a good idea?"

"Yes, Ellie," Daddy replied, "I think that would be a very good idea. You could earn more money there that you could put into savings for whatever does come next in your life, than you could if you worked at almost any other store. And, Wannamaker's really is a good department store."

After Daddy finished saying what he was saying to Ellie, he turned to Junior and asked him how his day went.

"Well," he began, "I had a great time at Mik's house. The first thing we did was clean his room."

"What?!" Mommy responded with a heap of surprise in her voice. "You never even want to clean your own room. Why did you boys clean his?"

"Because," Junior replied, quite matter-of-factly, "his mom told us that we could not play with anything until he cleaned his room. So, he did, and I helped him. It was better than just sitting around doing nothing would have been."

Then, after the chuckles from the rest of the family stopped, Junior continued with, "After we were done with that, we played a bunch of different games. We started with Battleship, and I won that one. Then we played Checkers and Mik won that one. Of course, that did not surprise me. I never seem to win at Checkers no matter who I am playing with. Next, we played Stratego, and we both won that one."

"How could you both win?" Maria asked with a hint of disbelief in her voice.

"They played two games," Ellie responded for Junior.

"How did you know that?" Junior asked, but not seriously. Afterall, that is what Ellie and Junior always did when they played Stratego.

"Seriously?" Ellie asked in a teasing tone. "How could I not know? We do it all the time."

"Yeah," Junior replied, with a smirk on his face and a tinge of laughter in his voice, "I guess we do."

After another brief pause so that he could take another bite of his shepherd's pie, he continued with,

"It was nice that we both won two games; that way neither of us had to feel bad. Of course, we did get a little frustrated when we had to put them away. It is always so much easier to make a mess than it is to clean one up."

Now, of course, that got a lot of chuckles from everyone, after which Daddy asked, "Did you do anything else besides playing games?

"Oh yeah," Junior said, "we also built a whole city with all of his Legos. Then, when we were done with that, we put together some model cars. That was really a lot of fun too! But that was not all we did. We spent most of our time just talking about this, that, and everything else."

"Well," Maria, who was next to share, began, "I did not do too much today. I just spent my time reading my Nancy Drew book. I really like those books."

"I am glad that you do! They are fun books to read," Mommy responded, and then shared her day's report. "I had a lot to do at work today."

Another **Side Note:** Mommy worked at a nursing home. She was one of the kitchen attendants who helped to cook the meals. But she was also patients' attendant. She helped them get in and out of bed, take bathroom breaks, get dressed, go to the lounge... well, just about anything the patients wanted or needed to do, she helped with. Okay, back to Mommy.

"It seemed that everyone needed more help than they usually do. And, we actually got several new tenants, so I had to prepare rooms for them. But it was still a good day. Everyone worked together, so everything that needed to get done, got done."

Daddy was the last one to share his daily report, and his was pretty short too. All he had to say was, "It was a typical work day for me. I walked my route, collecting my client's insurance payments, and now, after dinner, I will balance my books."

Now, even though everyone had shared their daily reports, the talking did not end until dinner ended. After all, the Stations were a family, a close family, an Italian family, so whenever they were together, they were always talking about this, that, everything else, and nothing at all.

After everyone was done eating, Jeannie, whose turn it was to clean up after dinner, started doing the dishes. After she cleaned off the table and the stove, and was done washing, drying, and putting the dishes away, she joined Mommy, who was resting comfortably in the corner seat of their comfy couch, watching "Adam 12."

Junior went to his room to put together another model; this one was a spaceship. And Maria went to her room to continue reading her Nancy Drew book.

Daddy went to his boffedice room to...

"Wait!!!" you are screaming, 'What is a boffedice room?' You want to know.

Well, this is what that is. A boffedice room is a room that is used as both a bedroom and an office. Naturally, Ellie was the one who created that name. She took the words bed and office and blended them together—b and then ed from bed and off and then ice from office—and came up with boffedice! So, now you know, and I am certain that, by now, you are not surprised, because you know, because I told you before that Ellie always loved to create words. Okay, back to the story.

Daddy went to balance his insurance book and, as was often the case, just so she could be with him, Ellie went too. But she did not just go and sit in his room. Nope! She went to help him.

She sat down on the floor, next to his desk, where he was sitting, put his insurance book on her lap, and read to him the numbers he had written down on the account pages of the people from whom he had collected payments. Then he recorded them on his accountant sheet, totaled them up, and put the sheet into the folder he used to keep all the reports, statements, pap... okay, you get it, everything he needed to take with him to his weekly meeting with the bosses.

By the time they were done, everyone else was in the living room watching "Columbo," so Daddy and Ellie went to join them. But before Ellie went downstairs, she went up to her room to get her notebook and pen so she could continue working on the story she had started a couple of weeks earlier and *a deck of cards,* just in case anyone was interested in playing Go Fish. Then she went down to the living room, sat on the floor next to Daddy's oversized, comfy chair, where he was sitting, and, as everyone else watched T.V., she worked on her story. Or did she?

As Ellie tried to work on her story, her thoughts kept derailing to the question that had consumed her mind earlier that day, in fact, just about the whole day, and that was, **what next?**

Again, she found herself thinking about and writing down all the things she had done, learned, experienced, di... well, you know, all that her life experiences, schooling, extra-curricular activities, le... okay, here I go again. Let me just move on and say that her mind kept drifting to all those things that had brought her to where she was at that present time in her life, all the while adding wonderment about where she would be going from there.

As she thought about the possibility of getting a job at John Wannamaker's, she also contemplated what she would do with the money she would be earning. Of course, there was no question that she would give some of it to Daddy and Mommy to help with whatever they needed help with, and to demonstrate her responsibleness. And there was also no question that she most definitely would save most of it; that was something Ellie always did—SAVE—and not just money. She saved books and horse figurines, lighthouses and teddy bears, bottles and rings, Jesus pictures and jewl... well, let me just say, she saved a lot of things. But she also had another thought. And that thought was this.

Ellie had always and forever wanted to learn how to ride a horse, not just take pony rides at fairs, but actually learn to ride a horse, a horse that she still believed was on the earth because she had asked God to put them here, because she loved them so much. Yes, you remember that how she always believed every horsey was her horsey. In fact, she never lost her love for horses; it just grew as she grew. Well, actually it grew more than she grew and she even thought she wanted to be a jockey and an equestrian. So, as she sat there, trying to work on her story, which, by the way, was about a horse, she decided she would use some of the money that she earned to pay for riding lessons. And that was what she did.

It only took her about a week to get a job at the John Wannamaker Department Store, and she began working the day after she got the job. Oh, and she was a floater, so she got to work in every department. Now, some of them like the toy department, the book department, and the games department, she really liked. But others, like the lingerie department, and the cosmetics department, she really did not like. In fact, so much did she not like working in those departments that she would have been very happy if they had disappeared from the store. Nonetheless, she was still very grateful for the opportunity that working in any department provided for her to earn the money that made it possible for her to finally take riding lessons. That is what she did at the Bar-T-L Ranch.

She had begun working at John Wannamaker's in the middle of June and then began riding lessons sometime in July. Now, while working at Wannamaker's was okay, better than it would have been anywhere else. At least, that is what she believed, it was her riding lessons at Bar-T-L Ranch that she absolutely loved, loved, loved!! And she apparently was a pretty natural rider because within just a few months, her instructor was entering her in equitation events, which she usually placed first or second in. They even had 'at the ranch' races, and Ellie typically came in first. Yes, Ellie was very good at riding and she had been given a horse to ride that was also very gifted. So, even though she still had many 'what next questions,' she felt she was actually on her way to... something, but she did not yet know exactly what that something was.

Ellie knew that even though she wanted what she had always wanted a home in the country and horses. She knew she wanted to forever and always continue learning, she still did not know exactly which direction to face nor what the end goal should be, because Ellie also knew that, more than anything else, she wanted to, and would do, whatever God wanted her to do, but she could not yet say she actually knew what that was.

You see, the more she studied the Bible and the history of the Catholic Church, the more certain she was becoming that becoming a nun was actually not the right choice. In fact, the more she studied, the more certain she was that she did not even have, and never even had, the truth. It seemed to her that what the Bible taught and what the church taught were not the same things. So, she continued looking into different things, talking to others to get their thoughts, and praying to God for His help to know what to do, what to decide, and how to do whatever it was that she needed to do in order to do what God wanted her to do. In fact, she told Him, "If there is truth in this world, and if Thou will lead me to it, I will live it, no matter what that means!"

Then, after a bit of a while and, many, many, ma... well, you understand, many prayers, in consequence to a truly unexpected realization that she really did not have God's true truth in her life. She found herself on a new path of discovery. She began searching for that truth and before too long, she realized that it was God, Himself, who had led her to that journey, which was leading her in a direction and to an end that would change her life in amazing, blessed ways. It was a journey most needed. It was *The Ticket* to all the best that **what next** could bring!

Now, of course, it was not a short journey, so there were still many other things that captured her attention. And, as was most definitely not a surprise to anyone, one of the most pleasing of those things was the horses that she had been given the opportunity to feed, care for, train, and ride at Bar T-L Ranch!

ABOUT THE AUTHOR

Eileen DiStasio-Clark is the second oldest of four children. She is the mother of eleven children and grandmother to twenty-three grandchildren, to date. As a member of The Church of Jesus Christ of Latter-Day Saints, she serves in various positions, teaching, leading, and ministering to children, youth, and adults. Currently, she is also a Family History Missionary. Eileen established the Pursuit of Excellence Institute of Family Education, a non-profit organization focused on strengthening the family. Presently she holds an A.A., a B.A., and an M.A. in Clinical Psychology and is working on the completion of her Doctoral Degree.